Discover Your Story

Finding Your Branding Themes

Kristen Arbour

Batch Your Story

~DEDICATION~

To all those who are a part of my story and to all of those that will be.

~CONTENTS~

Discover Your Story

~FOREWARD~

Who needs to hear your story?

This workbook will help you outline and design the story that you tell the world.

Whether it is on your social media, your website, or in your next book; well-crafted images that tell the story of you are very important.

It is said "A picture is worth a thousand words." By following Kristen's system your pictures will touch and inspire thousands of people with your story.

Kristen helps you investigate how to best serve your client and build your business through focusing on who they are and how to best assist them in getting what they desire in life.

After completing this book, you will have well-crafted themes to share with those you serve.

-Tamia Dow
International Award-Winning, Best-Selling Author of
"In Celebration of You,
Fun Activities to Help Rediscover You"
WWW.TAMIADOW.COM

~INTRODUCTION~

As a personal brand photographer, I capture my clients' stories. Before the image can be captured the story has to be discovered. This workbook has been designed to help you discover your branding story.
Once you know your story, you can tell it better.

My "WHAT" is story-based images for entrepreneurs and influencers.

1
~THE WHAT~

Every story has a subject. Your story has several important subjects. You, your client, and what you offer are all key subjects in your branding story. This chapter focuses on the what, that is, the what you offer. Whether it is a product, a service, or an experience the following questions will put your what into words. Your description will shape your story and the direction it takes. We will refer to this section throughout the book. How you describe the what you offer will give a peek at who you are and your values.

Describe your product or service.

_____

_____

_____

_____

_____

_____

How is your product/service used?

_____

_____

_____

_____

_____

_____

What problem does it solve?

_____

_____

_____

_____

_____

_____

What are the top 3 things you want others to know about your product/ service?

1._____

_____

2._____

_____

3._____

_____

What is your favorite thing about your product/ service?

_____

_____

_____

_____

_____

_____

How do you deliver your product/ service?

_____

_____

_____

_____

_____

_____

What are your goals for your product/ service?

_____

_____

_____

_____

_____

_____

_____

How often does an individual need to buy your product/ service?

_____

_____

_____

_____

_____

_____

How do you feel about your product/ service?

_____

_____

_____

_____

_____

_____

_____

What makes your product/ service different than others?

_____

_____

_____

_____

_____

_____

How do others describe your product / service?

_____

_____

_____

_____

_____

_____

_____

We can learn a lot about how we are presenting our product/ service by listening to how others describe it. There are four types of people whose description of your product/service can let you see the message you are sending.

- ❖ The Uninformed - those you have not yet educated about your product/service
- ❖ The Prospect- those you have educated but have not purchased
- ❖ The Client- those who have purchased
- ❖ The Raving Fan- those who tell others about your product/service

The following pages give you questions so you can see how the different types of people understand your what. I encourage you to ask at least three people of each type.

Uninformed #1

Name: _____

What have you heard about (product/service)?

_____

_____

_____

Do you have any questions about (product/service)?

_____

_____

_____

Do you think that (product/service) is something that would benefit you? Why or why not?

_____

_____

_____

_____

_____

Would you like to learn more about (product/service)?

Uninformed #2

Name: _____

What have you heard about (product/service)?

_____

_____

_____

Do you have any questions about (product/service)?

_____

_____

_____

Do you think that (product/service) is something that would benefit you? Why or why not?

_____

_____

_____

_____

Would you like to learn more about (product/service)?

Uninformed #3

Name: _____

What have you heard about (product/service)?

_____

_____

_____

_____

Do you have any questions about (product/service)?

_____

_____

_____

_____

Do you think that (product/service) is something that would benefit you? Why or why not?

_____

_____

_____

_____

_____

Would you like to learn more about (product/service)?

Prospect #1

Name: _____

How would you describe (product/service)?

_____

_____

_____

Do you have any questions about (product/service)?

_____

_____

_____

Do you think that (product/service) is something that would benefit you? If it would why haven't you invested in it? If it wouldn't, why not?

_____

_____

_____

_____

_____

Would you like to learn more about (product/service)?

Prospect #2

Name: _____

How would you describe (product/service)?

_____

_____

_____

_____

Do you have any questions about (product/service)?

_____

_____

_____

_____

Do you think that (product/service) is something that would benefit you? If it would why haven't you invested in it? If it wouldn't, why not?

_____

_____

_____

_____

_____

_____

Would you like to learn more about (product/service)?

Prospect #3

Name: _____

How would you describe (product/service)?

_____

_____

_____

_____

Do you have any questions about (product/service)?

_____

_____

_____

_____

Do you think that (product/service) is something that would benefit you? If it would why haven't you invested in it? If it wouldn't, why not?

_____

_____

_____

_____

_____

Would you like to learn more about (product/service)?

Client #1

Name: _____

How would you describe (product/service)?

_____

_____

_____

_____

How would you describe your experience with (product/service)?

_____

_____

_____

_____

Would you recommend (product/service)? Why or why not?

_____

_____

_____

_____

_____

_____

Client #2

Name: _____

How would you describe (product/service)?

_____

_____

_____

How would you describe your experience with (product/service)?

_____

_____

_____

Would you recommend (product/service)? Why or why not?

_____

_____

_____

_____

_____

Client #3

Name: _____

How would you describe (product/service)?

_____

_____

_____

How would you describe your experience with (product/service)?

_____

_____

_____

Would you recommend (product/service)? Why or why not?

_____

_____

_____

_____

_____

_____

Raving Fan #1

Name: _____

How would you describe (product/service)?

_____

_____

_____

_____

How would you describe your experience with (product/service)?

_____

_____

_____

_____

Why do you recommend (product/service)?

_____

_____

_____

_____

_____

_____

_____

Raving Fan #2

Name: _____

How would you describe (product/service)?

_____

_____

_____

_____

How would you describe your experience with (product/service)?

_____

_____

_____

_____

Why do you recommend (product/service)?

_____

_____

_____

_____

_____

_____

_____

Raving Fan #3

Name: _____

How would you describe (product/service)?

_____

_____

_____

_____

How would you describe your experience with
(product/service)?

_____

_____

_____

_____

Why do you recommend (product/service)?

_____

_____

_____

_____

_____

_____

Evaluate

How would you feel about how others describe (product/service)?

_____

_____

_____

_____

Is there something you would change about how you describe your (product/service) after you heard their descriptions?

_____

_____

_____

_____

What did their descriptions show that they value about your (product/service)?

_____

_____

_____

_____

_____

My "WHO" uses images to share their story and build connections.

2
~THE WHO~

When writing a story an author will often make an outline of the details of each main character. Doing the same for your ideal client can help you communicate with them. The following questions will help you identify your audience in more detail. The better you understand who your client is the stronger the connection you can make with them.

What is the first thing that comes to mind when you are asked who is your client?

_____

_____

_____

_____

_____

_____

Can you describe your client without using the words someone or anyone?

_____

_____

_____

_____

_____

_____

What problem does your client have?

_____

_____

_____

_____

_____

_____

What do you have in common with your client?

_____

_____

_____

_____

_____

_____

What is the age range and gender of your client?

_____

_____

_____

_____

_____

_____

Does your client work in a specific industry?

_____

_____

_____

_____

_____

_____

Does your client have specific hobbies or interests?

_____

_____

_____

_____

_____

_____

Where does your client shop?

_____

_____

_____

_____

_____

_____

What is important to your client?

_____

_____

_____

_____

_____

_____

What are your clients core values?

_____

_____

_____

_____

_____

_____

What does your client do for fun or to relax?

_____

_____

_____

_____

_____

_____

How would you describe your client's style of clothes?

_____

_____

_____

_____

_____

_____

What types of food does your client eat or avoid?

_____

_____

_____

_____

_____

_____

Any other important details about your client?

_____

_____

_____

_____

_____

_____

Check your character outline against real people. Interview at least three people who you view as ideal clients even if they are not actual clients.

Ideal Client #1

Name:_____

Age:_____

Gender:_____

Industry:_____

Problem:_____

_____

_____

Shop:_____

Hobbies:_____

_____

_____

Values:_____

_____

_____

Relax or unwind : _____

_____

_____

What they value most about your product/service:

_____

_____

_____

Ideal Client #2

Name:_____

Age:_____

Gender:_____

Industry:_____

Problem:_____

_____

_____

Shop:_____

Hobbies:_____

_____

_____

Values:_____

_____

_____

Relax or unwind : _____

_____

_____

What they value most about your product/service:

_____

_____

_____

Ideal Client #3

Name:_____

Age:_____

Gender:_____

Industry:_____

Problem:_____

_____

_____

Shop:_____

Hobbies:_____

_____

_____

Values:_____

_____

_____

Relax or unwind : _____

_____

_____

What they value most about your product/service:

_____

_____

_____

Who we see as our ideal client and those who are our raving fans are not always the same people. Interview at least three raving fans and see how their answers compare.

Raving Fan #1

Name:_____

Age:_____

Gender:_____

Industry:_____

Problem:_____

_____

_____

Shop:_____

Hobbies:_____

_____

_____

Values:_____

_____

_____

Relax or unwind : _____

_____

_____

What they value most about your product/service:

_____

_____

_____

Raving Fan #2

Name:_____

Age:_____

Gender:_____

Industry:_____

Problem:_____

_____

_____

Shop:_____

Hobbies:_____

_____

_____

Values:_____

_____

_____

Relax or unwind : _____

_____

_____

What they value most about your product/service:

_____

_____

_____

Raving Fan #3

Name:_____

Age:_____

Gender:_____

Industry:_____

Problem:_____

_____

_____

Shop:_____

Hobbies:_____

_____

_____

Values:_____

_____

_____

Relax or unwind : _____

_____

_____

What they value most about your product/service:

_____

_____

_____

What are the similarities and differences between your character outline, your ideal client interviews, and your raving fan interviews?

_____

_____

_____

_____

_____

_____

What did you find the most interesting takeaway from the interviews? Does it change who you think is your ideal client is?

_____

_____

_____

_____

_____

_____

My family is not my only "WHY", but they are a part of all my whys.

3
~THE WHY~

In a story the why is what motivates the characters. It is what pushes them to succeed when they are on the brink of failure. Their why forces them to stand up and find a way no matter how many times they fall. The why is bigger than the situation. Your why is what drives your branding story. It is one of the key elements that sets you apart from someone offering a similar product or service.

In the following questions we will look at your whys. We will start with the easier small whys and work our way to the bigger underlying why beneath the surface.

What is your first thought when someone asks you what your why is?

_____

_____

_____

_____

_____

_____

Is your first thought the one you share?

_____

_____

_____

_____

_____

_____

Refer to your responses in chapter 1 to answer the following questions.

Why do you offer your product/service?

_____

_____

_____

_____

_____

_____

Why do you solve the problem you described on page 3?

_____

_____

_____

_____

_____

_____

Look back to your goals for your product/ service on page 5. Why are those your goals?

_____

_____

_____

_____

_____

_____

What other goals do you have for your business?

_____

_____

_____

_____

_____

_____

What are your non-business goals?

_____

_____

_____

_____

_____

_____

Do your business and non-business goals have common motivation?

_____

_____

_____

_____

_____

_____

Use your client descriptions in chapter 2 to answer the following questions.

Why is this your client?

_____

_____

_____

_____

_____

_____

Why do you want to solve their problem?

_____

_____

_____

_____

_____

_____

Why do they want to have this problem solved?

_____

_____

_____

_____

_____

_____

Why do they want and/or need to work specifically with you?

_____

_____

_____

_____

_____

_____

What motivates your client? What is their why?

_____

_____

_____

_____

_____

_____

Why are you connected to your client?

_____

_____

_____

_____

_____

_____

It's easy to guess or assume that we know why someone does something. What we assume people are motivated by tells us more about us then them. By asking questions we not only create a deeper connection, but a better understanding of their why as well. I recommend asking at least one ideal client, one raving fan, and your followers on at least one social media platform the following questions.

Name: _____

What problem does my product/service solve for you?

_____

_____

_____

Why is it important for you to have this problem solved?_____

_____

_____

_____

Why work with me rather than someone else who offers a similar product/service?

_____

_____

_____

Name: _____
What problem does my product/service solve for you?

_____

_____

_____

Why is it important for you to have this problem
solved?_____

_____

_____

_____

_____

Why work with me rather than someone else who
offers a similar product/service?

_____

_____

_____

Name: _____

What problem does my product/service solve for you?

_____
_____
_____

Why is it important for you to have this problem
solved?_____

_____
_____
_____

Why work with me rather than someone else who
offers a similar product/service?

_____
_____
_____

Look at what motivates you in the following questions.

What pushes you to succeed?

_____

_____

_____

_____

_____

_____

What gets you going on a bad day?

_____

_____

_____

_____

_____

_____

What do you protect or fight for?

_____

_____

_____

_____

_____

_____

What causes or charities do you support?

_____

_____

_____

_____

_____

_____

Look for your bigger why's. Rate each item 0-5 on how important they are to you.

0 = not important

5 = very important

Add your own to the bottom

freedom	family
security	making a difference
time	changing the world
energy	leaving an impact
wealth	faith
fame	helping others
travel	experiences

I am not perfect, but it's my imperfections that make me valuable.

4
~I AM...~

You are the most important character in your branding story. People want to connect with you and your story. In this chapter we will look at you, your accomplishments, and your character traits. Having an outline of your personal details will make it easier to communicate who you are to others. It will also make it easier to see things you have in common with your client.

Name:_____

Title:_____

Age:_____

Gender:_____

Industry: _____

Shop for Food:_____

Shop for Clothes:_____

Shop for Necessities:_____

Shop for Luxuries:_____

How would you describe yourself?

_____

_____

_____

_____

_____

_____

What have you accomplished?

_____

_____

_____

_____

_____

_____

What awards have you received?

_____

_____

_____

_____

_____

_____

What are your hobbies?

_____

_____

_____

_____

_____

_____

What do you like to do to relax?

_____

_____

_____

_____

_____

_____

The next two boxes should be filled out at the same time as they are two sides of the same coin. It is important to outline both as they are key to who we are and how we want to be known.

I am _____

I am _____

I am _____

I am _____

I am _____

I am _____

I am _____

I am _____

I am _____

I am _____

I am _____

I am _____

I am _____

I am _____

I am _____

We often have stronger feelings about who we are not. We are quicker to defend ourselves and say that is not who I am than we are to recognize and claim who we are. For each I am not make sure you have a corresponding I am.

I am not _____

I am not _____

I am not _____

I am not _____

I am not _____

I am not _____

I am not _____

I am not _____

I am not _____

I am not _____

I am not _____

I am not _____

I am not _____

I am not _____

I am not _____

Describe your family?

_____

_____

_____

_____

_____

_____

What do you believe in?

_____

_____

_____

_____

_____

_____

What organizations, clubs, and groups do you belong to?

_____

_____

_____

_____

_____

_____

Do you donate your time, talent, or money somewhere?

_____

_____

_____

_____

_____

_____

How we think of ourselves and how others see us does not always lineup. Often, we put up masks that send different messages or fail to recognize positive character traits we have. Ask at least three people how they see you. *Note*- the last question is not there for you to change yourself but to inspire ideas on how to connect to your clients

Name: _____

How would you describe me?

_____

_____

_____

How would you describe what I offer?

_____

_____

_____

What are my best qualities?

1._____

2._____

3._____

What is something I could improve on?

_____

_____

Name: _____

How would you describe me?

_____

_____

_____

How would you describe what I offer?

_____

_____

_____

What are my best qualities?

1._____

2._____

3._____

What is something I could improve on?

_____

_____

Name: _____

How would you describe me?

_____

_____

_____

How would you describe what I offer?

_____

_____

_____

What are my best qualities?

1._____

2._____

3._____

What is something I could improve on?

_____

_____

How do you feel about how others describe you and what you offer?

_____

_____

_____

_____

_____

_____

What do you think of what they listed as your best qualities?

_____

_____

_____

_____

_____

_____

Do you think the area you could improve on is
accurate? Why or why not?

_____

_____

_____

_____

_____

_____

Does your ideal client have this common with you?

_____

_____

_____

_____

_____

_____

My faith is very connected to my core values.

5
~CORE VALUES
AND PERSONAL CREED~

Even deeper than your why, your core values motivate your actions. Having a clear idea of your core values can guide your choices and grow your connections. They give you something to check your decisions with. If you find that your decisions and core values don't line up, you need to figure out if those are really your values. Something is not your core value just because you want it to be, or because you like the concept. Core values are values you are willing to make sacrifices for. In this chapter we will start with everyday things we value and work our way to a personal creed we can stand by.

What do you value or look for in items you own?

Rate each item 0-5 on how important they are to you.

0 = not important

5 = very important

Add your own to the bottom

quality	uniqueness
function	form
price	solution it provides
How long it will last	value
popularity	beauty
ease of use	sophistication

What do you value or look for in services you use?

Rate each item 0-5 on how important they are to you.

0 = not important

5 = very important

Add your own to the bottom

quality	uniqueness
function	speed
price	solution it provides
time	value
popularity	knowledge

What do you value or look for in ways you spend your time?

Rate each item 0-5 on how important they are to you.

0 = not important

5 = very important

Add your own to the bottom

money making	creative endeavors
restful activities	having fun
education	entertainment
social media	outdoors
building relationships	enjoying beauty

What do you value or look for in people you build relationships with?

Rate each item 0-5 on how important they are to you.

0 = not important

5 = very important

Add your own to the bottom

quality of character	trustworthiness
mutual interests	responsible
authenticity	solution they provide
honesty	fun
popularity	beauty

What do you consider your core values?

Rate each item 0-5 on how important they are to you.

0 = not important

5 = very important

Do you hold yourself to your core values to guide your choices and lifestyle?

_____

_____

_____

_____

Organizations and clubs sometimes have creeds to establish agreed upon beliefs, standards, or goals. The next several questions will look at creeds you already hold yourself to.

Do you belong to any group that has a creed? If not is there a group that you admire or follow that has a creed?

_____

_____

_____

_____

_____

_____

_____

_____

_____

Do the creeds influence your choices or are they just words to you?

_____

_____

_____

_____

_____

_____

What are some ways you can see the creed in your life? (ex. because I hold myself to _____ I choose to _____)

_____

_____

_____

_____

_____

_____

Were there creeds that you held to when you were
younger that left an impact in your life?

_____

_____

_____

_____

_____

_____

Do you have a person you admire that lives by a
creed?

_____

_____

_____

_____

_____

_____

Everyone has things they strongly believe in. These are things you already make decisions based on. They could be faith based, relationship based (how you believe you and others should be treated), or cause and effect based. Most likely you will have beliefs from more than one base.

Core Beliefs (3-7)

1._____

_____

2._____

_____

3._____

_____

4._____

_____

5._____

_____

6._____

_____

7._____

_____

Core qualities are like branding, they are what you want people saying about your character when you are not in the room. They can be a combination of qualities you already have and ones you are working on acquiring. Core qualities must be important enough to you that you would make sacrifices for them to be true.

Core Qualities (3-7)

1._____

_____

2._____

_____

3._____

_____

4._____

_____

5._____

_____

6._____

_____

7._____

_____

Usually you want your goals to be as specific as possible. The goal of these goals is to create a measuring stick for branding decisions. You want them to be able to be always true about who you are and what you stand for. They are how you choose to put your core beliefs and core qualities into action.

Core Goals (3-7)

1._____

_____

2._____

_____

3._____

_____

4._____

_____

5._____

_____

6._____

_____

7._____

_____

Write your own personal creed. Make it something you believe in and can hold yourself to. Your personal creed is a promise to yourself to be true to your core elements. You can use the following to start sentences in your creed
* I am
* I promise to
* I commit to
* I believe (in or the following to be true)

Personal Creed

_____

_____

_____

_____

_____

_____

_____

_____

_____

_____

_____

_____

_____

_____

My themes, like my photos, are framed by how I see the world.

6
~THEMES~

Themes are the heart of your message. They are the common thread that weaves your short stories into a larger tapestry. Your branding story has three to seven themes. In this chapter we will refer to the past chapters and identify topics in common.

A three-legged stool and a cord of three strands are used as examples of strength and stability. Having at least three themes gives your branding story similar stability. Your first three themes are like primary colors, they are essential to paint the picture of your brand. Look for words, phrases, and ideas that you have in common with your client to create themes that will make the strongest connection. I have left room in the boxes for you to brainstorm several possible themes in each category.

Theme based on the problem you solve:

_____

_____

_____

_____

_____

_____

Theme based on the your why:

_____

_____

_____

_____

_____

_____

Theme based on your core values or personal creed:

_____

_____

_____

_____

_____

_____

The following boxes give you more ideas for themes and a place to brainstorm. Refer to past chapters to find things you share with your client.

Theme based on a shared interest or hobby:

_____

_____

_____

_____

_____

_____

Theme based on a shared way to relax or unwind:

_____

_____

_____

_____

_____

_____

Theme based on a shared problem or stressor:

_____

_____

_____

_____

_____

_____

Theme based on a shared belief:

_____

_____

_____

_____

_____

_____

Theme based on a shared quality:

_____

_____

_____

_____

_____

_____

Theme based on shared goals:

_____

_____

_____

_____

_____

_____

Theme based on posts that have gotten good response:

_____

_____

_____

_____

_____

_____

Other Theme Ideas:

_____

_____

_____

_____

_____

_____

Where you need to have at least three themes, you don't want to have more than seven. Think of it like a rainbow. You can make a rainbow with just the three primary colors. When you look at a rainbow you see seven colors. More than seven themes cause the colors to fade together and lose their impact.

Themes (3-7)

1.(based on the problem you solve)

_____

_____

2.(based on your why)

_____

_____

3.(based on your core values or personal creed)

_____

_____

4._____

_____

5._____

_____

6._____

_____

7._____

_____

From my clothes to my decor, my style is conservative and quirky.

7
~PERSONAL STYLE~

What you wear and how you decorate your home and office are a part of your story. It is a visual reflection of who you are. In a culture where so much of our time is spent on social media, selfies and snapshots tend to define us. Tell a better story by being aware of how your clothing and decor are the illustrations in your branding story.

Describe your style of clothes:

_____

_____

_____

_____

_____

_____

How is your style of clothes similar and/or different from your client's style?

_____

_____

_____

_____

_____

_____

How does your style of clothes reflect who you are?

_____

_____

_____

_____

_____

_____

How does your style of clothes reflect your values?

_____

_____

_____

_____

_____

_____

Picture or description of your favorite outfit:

_____

_____

_____

_____

_____

_____

Why is this your favorite outfit?

_____

_____

_____

_____

_____

_____

Describe your style of home decor:

_____

_____

_____

_____

_____

_____

How is your style of home decor similar and/or different from your client's style?

_____

_____

_____

_____

_____

_____

How does your style of home decor reflect who you are?

_____

_____

_____

_____

_____

_____

How does your style of home decor reflect your values?

_____

_____

_____

_____

_____

_____

What decorations or design elements are most important to you?

_____

_____

_____

_____

_____

_____

Why are they important to you?

_____

_____

_____

_____

_____

_____

I define my story my story by deciding what to share.

~OWN YOUR STORY~

In this workbook you have discovered the who, what, and why of your branding story. You have found your themes and considered the clothes and stage of your characters. You are ready to "Define Your Story". The next book in this series uses what we have discovered in this book to create a clear outline for all your branding needs. Whether you are doing your branding and social media yourself or working with a strategist and/or social media manager, "Define Your Story" brings clarity to your message.

~ABOUT THE AUTHOR~

KRISTEN ARBOUR

Kristen Arbour is an internationally published photographer, author, playwright, educator, and speaker. She specializes in Personal Brand Photography and captures her clients' unique stories in pictures. Find out how you can work with her at BatchYourStory.com

www.ingramcontent.com/pod-product-compliance
Lightning Source LLC
Chambersburg PA
CBHW072156170526
45158CB00004BA/1674